D0772728

MONUMENTAL MILESTONES
GREAT EVENTS OF MODERN TIMES

The Assassination of John F. Kennedy, 1963

President Kennedy in a rocker in the Yellow Oval Room in the White House.

PUBLISHERS

P.O. Box 196
Hockessin, Delaware 19707

Titles in the Series

MONUMENTAL MILESTONES
GREAT EVENTS OF MODERN TIMES

The Assassination of John F. Kennedy, 1963

John F. Kennedy with Jackie and their two children, John Jr. and Caroline, in 1962.

Susan Sales Harkins and
William H. Harkins

Printing   1   2   3   4   5   6   7   8   9

Library of Congress Cataloging-in-Publication Data
Harkins, Susan Sales.
    The assassination of John F. Kennedy, 1963 / by Susan Sales Harkins and
    William H. Harkins.
        p. cm. — (Monumental milestones)
    Includes bibliographical references and index.
    ISBN 978-1-58415-540-9 (library bound) 39535389   2/09
    1. Kennedy, John F. (John Fitzgerald), 1916–1963—Assassination—Juvenile
literature. I. Harkins, William H. II. Title.
E842.9.H29 2008
973.922092—dc22
                                                                                2007000774

ABOUT THE AUTHORS: Susan and William Harkins live in Kentucky, where they enjoy writing together for children. Susan has written many books for adults and children. William is a history buff. In addition to writing, he is a member of the Air National Guard.

PHOTO CREDITS: Cover, pp. 10, 17—Tom Dillard/*The Dallas Morning News*; p. 1—Robert Knudson/John F. Kennedy Presidential Library and Museum; pp. 3, 11, 12, 16, 26—Cecil Stoughton/John F. Kennedy Presidential Library and Museum; pp. 6, 38, 41—U.S. National Archives and Records Administration; pp. 18, 20—*The Dallas Morning News*; p. 22—Ike Altgens/Associated Press; pp. 24, 28—Associated Press; p. 31—Bob Jackson/*Dallas Herald-Times*; p. 33—Dallas Police Department; p. 34—Abbie Rowe/John F. Kennedy Presidential Library and Museum.

PUBLISHER'S NOTE: This story is based on the authors' extensive research, which they believe to be accurate. Documentation of such research is contained on page 47.

    The internet sites referenced herein were active as of the publication date. Due to the fleeting nature of some web sites, we cannot guarantee they will all be active when you are reading this book.

                                                                                PPC

Contents

The Assassination of JFK

Susan Sales Harkins and William H. Harkins

*For Your Information

WANTED

FOR

TREASON

THIS MAN is wanted for treasonous activities against the United States:

1. **Betraying the Constitution (which he swore to uphold):**
He is turning the sovereignty of the U. S. over to the communist controlled United Nations.
He is betraying our friends (Cuba, Katanga, Portugal) and befriending our enemies (Russia, Yugoslavia, Poland).

2. He has been WRONG on innumerable issues affecting the security of the U.S. (United Nations-Berlin wall-Missile removal-Cuba-Wheat deals-Test Ban Treaty, etc.)

3. He has been lax in enforcing Communist Registration laws.

4. He has given support and encouragement to the Communist inspired racial riots.

5. He has illegally invaded a sovereign State with federal troops.

6. He has consistantly appointed Anti-Christians to Federal office: Upholds the Supreme Court in its Anti-Christian rulings.
Aliens and known Communists abound in Federal offices.

7. He has been caught in fantastic LIES to the American people (including personal ones like his previous marraige and divorce).

This circular was passed around Dallas before and during Kennedy's fateful trip.

Some Americans strongly opposed Kennedy's policies on civil rights and the minimum wage. However, he was also loved by many, and his assassination seemed unthinkable.

A Minute in Dallas

Secret Service Agent Forrest Sorrels studied the crowd ahead as the president's motorcade passed Dealey Plaza on Houston Street. Forrest was the agent in charge of Dallas. He'd spent the last three weeks preparing for the president's visit, and he was anxious.

Shielding his eyes from the noonday sun, Forrest scanned the redbrick façade of the Texas School Book Depository looming straight ahead. Some spectators were standing at open windows and cheering. Everything looked secure, but he was glad it was almost over.

The lead car turned left onto Elm Street. In just a few more minutes, the motorcade would take the highway to the Trade Mart, where the president would give a speech.

Inside the presidential limousine, President Kennedy smiled and waved at the crowd. Dallas surprised him. He had anticipated smaller crowds and maybe even protesters. Many Texans were at odds with his goals for the country. Just the day before, an anti-Kennedy group had distributed circulars with Kennedy's picture and the words *WANTED FOR TREASON*.

Southerners, and that included Texans, didn't agree with the president's views on civil rights. Nearly a century after the Civil War, some Texans still supported forced segregation. The president also hoped to pass a minimum wage law. Poor Texans didn't see how a rich man from the Northeast could understand their needs.

Many Texans didn't like President Kennedy, and yet a quarter of a million people were cheering the motorcade. He was definitely surprised and delighted with the way the trip was going, even if it was hotter than expected. Mrs. Kennedy was wearing a wool suit because the forecast had called for

cooler weather. The ride was exciting, but she would be glad to get out of the sun.

Just ahead, the clock on the Book Depository said 12:30. The president's car turned left onto Elm Street.

Amos Lee Euins, just fifteen, stood on Elm Street opposite the Book Depository. He waved at President Kennedy, who waved back. The teenager rolled his eyes upward in disbelief—had President Kennedy really waved at him? He saw a pipe hanging from a window of the Book Depository. It was odd, he thought, but he quickly returned his gaze to the president.

Across the street, Mrs. Donald Baker jumped back in alarm when she saw tiny chips of concrete shoot upward from behind the president's car. Just then, President Kennedy raised his hands as something sprayed his face. Across the square, James Tague felt something fine pepper his cheek just as something exploded at the curb.

A loud *crack* echoed through the square.

The crowd froze.

Instinctively, Texas Governor John B. Connally turned right, toward the sound. As a hunter, he recognized that sound: Someone had just shot a rifle! Quickly, he turned left to check the president sitting behind him.

On the fifth floor of the Book Depository, employee Hank Norman was watching the motorcade when he thought he heard a shot from the floor above. "Someone is firing from upstairs right over my head," he thought.[1] He heard the quiet clank of what sounded like a shell casing striking the floor above. The Book Depository was an old building. You could see through the cracks in the floorboards. It wasn't unusual for employees to hear noises from overhead.

S. M. Holland stood on the triple underpass that crossed Elm Street and watched the motorcade. It was coming his way. He thought he heard a firecracker. Was that a puff of smoke rising from the stockade fence on the grassy knoll?

In the vice president's car, Secret Service Agent Rufus Youngblood heard the noise and yelled, "Get down!"[2] He shoved the vice president down and sat on him, acting as a human shield.

Then a second *crack* exploded. This time, the bullet hit flesh, plunging through the president's right shoulder just below his neck. The bullet passed

through his trachea and exited at the base of his throat, nicking the knot in his blue silk tie. The speeding bullet then traveled a few feet until it slammed into Governor Connally's back. It exited through his chest, ricocheted off his raised right wrist, and finally pierced his left thigh.

"We are hit!"[3] yelled Secret Service Agent Roy Kellerman from the front seat. William Greer, the agent driving the car, hit the brake. President Kennedy reached for his throat with both hands. "What are they doing to you?" screamed Mrs. Kennedy.[4] The president slumped toward her.

Spectators in the crowd scattered for safety. Some fell to the ground and covered their heads. A siren began to wail.

Governor Connally looked down at the blood gushing from his chest. Mrs. Connally pulled him close to her.

In the follow-up car, Agent George Hickey stood up with an AR-15 rifle, but he didn't shoot. He couldn't find a target. Agent Clint Hill was assigned to protect the First Lady. He was riding on the left running board of the follow-up car. When he saw the confusion in the backseat of the presidential limousine, he jumped down and raced toward the president's car.

Crack! A third explosion ripped through the plaza.

Stunned, Mrs. Kennedy watched as a third bullet shattered her husband's skull. In horror, she watched a piece of his head fly backward into the street. A larger piece fell onto the seat, just beside him. Blood spurted from the severed arteries in his brain.

Governor Connally heard the shot. He knew by the sound of impact that it had struck the president.

"They have shot his head off," Mrs. Kennedy screamed. "I have his brains on my hand."[5]

In shock, Mrs. Kennedy climbed out onto the trunk of the car. By this time, Agent Hill had reached the back of the car. He grasped the special handrail on the trunk with one hand. With his free hand, he shoved Mrs. Kennedy back into the car as it sped away.

Hill pulled himself onto the trunk and peered into the backseat. He was unprepared for what he saw. President Kennedy's head lay upon some roses. His eyes were open, but the right side of his head was gone. Glancing about, Hill could see brain tissue smattered everywhere.

Agent Clint Hill rides on the running board of the follow-up car. He was responsible for keeping Jackie Kennedy safe.

Hill managed to climb onto the limousine just after the third bullet struck John F. Kennedy in the head. He used his body to shield the First Lady and the dead president as the car raced to the hospital.

Mrs. Kennedy said to Hill, "They have shot his head off."[6]

Hill pounded the trunk of the car with his fist. He turned back to look for the follow-up car, which was close behind. He turned his thumb downward. Those following knew immediately that President Kennedy was dying or already dead.

President Kennedy's "New Frontier" platform was ambitious. His goals included the following:

- A higher minimum wage.
- Medical care for the elderly.
- Increased federal aid for education.
- Civil rights legislation to protect individual freedoms, including legislation to make forced segregation illegal.
- Major tax cuts, especially for the poor.
- Increased defense spending in the hopes of ending the cold war— the dispute that began after World War II between Western countries such as the United States and England and Eastern Europe.

Kennedy succeeded in getting an increase to the hourly minimum wage. In 1961, the minimum wage increased by 15 percent, from $1.00 to $1.15, and then in 1963 by nearly 9 percent, from $1.15 to $1.25.[7] Congress also agreed to spend more money on weapons.

Those first few years in office, President Kennedy didn't push hard for the other reforms. He hoped to win Congress over during his first term. Then, if he were reelected in 1964 to a second term, he planned to aggressively push civil rights legislation and other social reforms.

Although not part of his official platform, President Kennedy also supported space exploration. He was eager for the United States to be the first nation to put a man on the moon.

Kennedy didn't live long enough to achieve many of his goals. President Lyndon B. Johnson's platform, the "Great Society," undertook most of Kennedy's social reforms, including civil rights.

Congress enacted the Civil Rights Act in 1964, which made discrimination illegal in government and employment. The Jim Crow laws in the South were suddenly illegal. That meant segregation in schools, housing, and hiring would be a crime.

Kennedy inspects the interior of the *Friendship 7* Mercury capsule with astronaut Colonel John Glenn, Jr.

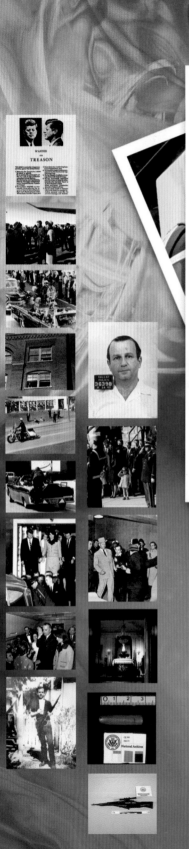

In Dallas, the wife of Mayor Earle Cabell presented Jackie with a bouquet of roses.

Within minutes of arriving in Dallas, President Kennedy's shattered and bloodied head lay upon the scattered rose blossoms his wife had received at the airport.

Friday Morning

Early on November 22, 1963, a young man sat alone drinking coffee in a Texas suburb. His wife had just returned to bed after getting up with their infant daughter, Rachel. She hoped to catch a short nap before June, her two-year-old daughter, got up for the day.

The man went into the bedroom and stood next to his sleepy wife. He told her to buy whatever she and the girls needed. He left some money for her in a wallet he kept in her dresser. Quietly, he also removed his wedding ring and placed it in a teacup.[1]

He walked quickly to the garage and unrolled a blanket, revealing a rifle hidden inside. Carefully, he wrapped the rifle in paper, making sure one end was thicker than the other. Then he rolled the blanket back up and returned it to the spot in the garage where he kept it. You couldn't tell just by looking at the blanket that the rifle was gone.

Through a cold morning mist, he walked down the street to Buell Wesley Frazier's house. The two men both worked at the Texas School Book Depository. The young man often rode to work with Frazier on Mondays after spending the weekend with his wife and girls, who lived with Ruth Paine in the town of Irving. During the week, he stayed in a rented room. Frazier would be surprised to see him on a Friday morning, but he wouldn't mind.

During the ride into work, Frazier asked his rider what he had rolled up in the paper. Lee Harvey Oswald replied, "Curtain rods."[2]

Across town, President Kennedy was staring out the window of his Hotel Texas suite in Fort Worth. No one had expected rain. The long-range forecast had predicted dry, cool weather. His wife, Jackie, had chosen a fashionable, yet practical, wool suit for the motorcade and luncheon in Dallas. If it

started to rain hard, they'd have to install the limousine's bubble top, a huge clear covering that shielded the president and his guests from the weather. He hoped they wouldn't need it. He liked being close to the crowd, and the bubble top got in the way. After all, it wasn't bulletproof; it just protected them from the weather. Even though he could see the crowd and the crowd could see him, it just wasn't the same.

There were about 500 men and women standing in the cold mist. It was barely 8:00 A.M. The president knew that most of the people were there to see Jackie. Everyone loved her. If he couldn't win over Texans, Jackie could.

Fortunately, Texans had been warm and gracious. He was pleased because he would need the state's electoral votes to be reelected in 1964.

President Kennedy had two speeches to make in Fort Worth, then he and Jackie would fly to Dallas. After a motorcade through the Dallas streets, he would make a luncheon speech. That evening, they would attend two cocktail parties in the capital city of Austin. Finally, they would slip away to Vice President Lyndon B. Johnson's ranch near Johnson City for two blissful days of rest.

Around 9:30 A.M., Kennedy greeted a group of laborers in the hotel's parking lot. As usual, the crowd loved him. For the Secret Service agents, the last-minute event was a nightmare. It was difficult to protect the president when he insisted on greeting the public without warning. After the short speech in the basement parking lot, Kennedy walked through the hotel's kitchen to his breakfast event.

Outside in the rain, the crowd had grown to 5,000 people. A little before 11:00 A.M., the president's motorcade eased through the cheering throng in the hotel parking lot and headed for Carswell Air Force Base. The air was damp and the temperature was rising. Mrs. Kennedy was probably hot in her wool suit, but she didn't complain.

Air Force One, the presidential jet, flew President and Mrs. Kennedy to Love Field in Dallas. Air Force Two carried Vice President Johnson, his wife, and their staff. A third jet carried members of the press.

They landed at 11:39 A.M. (Love Field in Dallas is just minutes away from the airfield in Fort Worth.) Mrs. Kennedy stepped off the plane first and the crowd roared. They screamed her name as if she were a Hollywood movie star. She was radiant in her pink suit and matching hat, and they loved her.

Mayor Earle Cabell and other Dallas officials greeted President and Mrs. Kennedy. The mayor's wife handed Mrs. Kennedy a bouquet of red roses. Nearby, a large group of bystanders cheered from behind a fence. The president and his wife walked over and shook hands with the crowd while the Secret Service agents scrambled to protect them.

After shaking several hands, President Kennedy stopped and squinted at the sun. He noticed that the rain had stopped, so they wouldn't need the bubble top.

Across the city of Dallas, employees left their jobs for lunch earlier than usual. They all hoped to get a good spot on the sidewalk along the motorcade's route. Slowly, they filed into the streets and waited. Most of the employees at the Book Depository stood right out front on Elm Street. A few waited at open windows.

Oswald took his lunch to the sixth floor. He stacked book cartons to create a wall behind a window. Then he stepped between the barricade of boxes and a southeast window. Although he was alone on the sixth floor, he needed the boxes to hide him in case anyone should pass by.

From the window, he had a clear view of Dealey Plaza. Just below him was the corner of Houston and Elm, where the motorcade would turn. He ate his fried chicken and waited.

Around 11:55 A.M., the motorcade left Love Field. Chief Jesse Curry of the Dallas police force drove the lead car. Sheriff Bill Decker and Secret Service agents Forrest Sorrels and Winston Lawson were passengers. Four motorcycles in front of the lead car helped to nudge the waiting crowd off the streets and onto the curb.

The presidential limousine, bearing the presidential standard and the American flag, followed the lead car. Secret Service Agent William Greer drove; Secret Service Agent Roy Kellerman sat in the front passenger seat. Governor Connally and his wife, Nellie, sat in the middle seat. President and Mrs. Kennedy rode in the backseat.

Four motorcycles followed close behind the president's limousine. The patrolmen had strict orders to remain behind the car and *not* to ride between the president and the people lining the streets. Kennedy liked to see the crowd. He understood that the patrolmen just wanted to protect him, but he didn't want them blocking his view of the crowd—or the crowd's view of him.

The next car carried Secret Service agents in dark suits. They all wore sunglasses and had short haircuts. These agents protected President Kennedy and the First Lady. Clint Hill, the agent assigned to Mrs. Kennedy, rode on the follow-up car's left running board. John Ready, the president's agent, rode on the right running board. Some agents sat in the backseat with automatic rifles; others sat in the middle seat with shotguns.

The agents were unhappy with the arrangement. They preferred to ride on the presidential limousine's bumper. However, President Kennedy didn't like the agents to ride so close. He knew the men had a job to do, but he didn't want them to be obvious to the crowd.

Vice President Johnson, Senator Ralph Yarborough, and their wives followed behind the car full of Secret Service agents. Next came the Dallas mayor, Earle Cabell, and his wife. The remaining vehicles, and there were

On November 22, 1963, the streets of Dallas were lined with people.

Despite the political friction, the citizens of Dallas wanted to catch a glimpse of the president and his popular young wife.

several, carried the press, photographers, White House staff, and congress-men. The cars stretched for over a half mile.

At Craddock Park, the presidential limousine stopped to greet a group of children. A few minutes later, Father Oscar Huber arrived just in time to see the back of the president's head.

The sun was hot, even though the temperature was mild at 68 degrees. Jackie put on a pair of sunglasses, but removed them at the president's re-quest. He let the Secret Service agents wear sunglasses, but he didn't wear them himself. Nor did he like Jackie to wear them in public. He thought sun-glasses hid a person's personality and emotions.[3]

Howard Brennan waited on a low wall opposite the Texas School Book Depository building, and studied the people waiting at the windows of the Depository. Below the top floor, he saw a slender man standing at a window with a rifle. He knew that police and Secret Service agents were everywhere.

Just a split second before a bullet struck him, President Kennedy was smiling and waving to the people of Dallas.

A photographer catches the last smile seen from President John F. Kennedy.

CHAPTER 2

The open window on the sixth floor is where Lee Harvey Oswald fired the gun that killed Kennedy.

Spectators peer from the fifth-story windows of the Texas School Book Depository.

Abraham Zapruder stood on the grassy knoll on Elm Street and focused his 8-millimeter movie camera on the street. Arnold Rowland, barely eighteen, saw what he thought was a Secret Service agent in a top window of the Book Depository. He noticed that the man's rifle was larger than a .22.

Jack Ruby was in the advertising office of the *Morning News,* a local newspaper. From several of the second-floor windows, he could have watched the motorcade, but he was too busy buying ad space for his nightclubs.

Slowly, the motorcade made its way down Houston Street and turned left onto Elm. Zapruder turned his camera toward the motorcade and began filming. As the president's limousine passed the grassy knoll to the right, Mrs. Connally turned to the president and said, "You can't say Dallas isn't friendly to you today."[4]

He smiled but never replied, because an assassin fired three bullets. Two hit President Kennedy, but it took only one to end his life.

Abraham Zapruder filmed the president's motorcade from the north side of Elm Street. His footage of John F. Kennedy's assassination is just twenty-six seconds long.

That same day, Zapruder made three copies of the film. He gave two of the copies to the Secret Service, which sent one to the FBI. Zapruder kept the third copy.

Life magazine purchased the original film the next day. Zapruder told the Warren Commission that *Life* paid him $25,000, although $25,000 was actually the first installment. The full amount was $150,000, according to the contract.[5]

The purchase meant that the public would see only what *Life* chose to publish. On November 29, 1963, *Life* magazine published thirty-one still pictures from the film. They didn't identify the images by any specific order or sequence.

Using the film to measure and time the event, federal investigators reenacted the assassination. They filmed their reenactments and then compared their films to the Zapruder film. By doing so, they determined that Kennedy and Connally were aligned just right when the second bullet hit, allowing a single bullet to wound them both.[6]

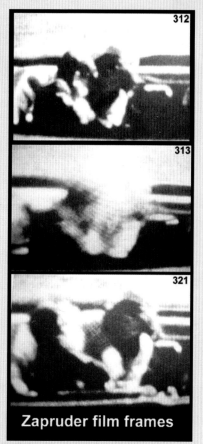

Zapruder film frames

Critics discovered that the first commission to study the assassination, the Warren Commission, worked with images from the Zapruder film that were out of sequence. What the commission saw reversed the president's reaction to the second bullet. Specifically, the images the commission used showed the force of the bullet throwing the president forward and then snapping backward. However, in the film, the president's head snaps backward first.[7] That means the bullet struck the front of his head. If the bullet hit the front of his head, there had to be more than one shooter, because Oswald was standing behind the president. Critics accused the Warren Commission of deliberately mishandling evidence.

A second commission, assigned in 1977 to reinvestigate the assassination, identified what they believed to be a fourth bullet.[8]

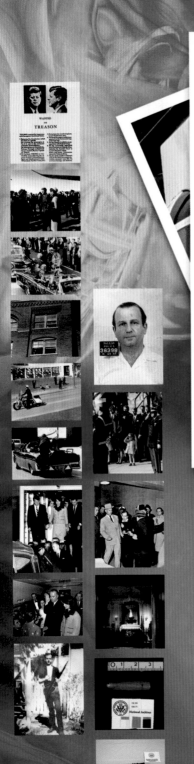

After hearing gunshots, spectators ran for cover while others dropped to the ground.

Reporters scrambled to take as many photographs as possible.

The Aftermath

Clint Hill clung to the back of the presidential limousine as it sped down the highway to Parkland Hospital. Jackie Kennedy cradled her husband's head in her lap. The president's right leg twitched involuntarily. A gurgling sound came from his throat wound.

In Dealey Plaza, people looked toward the Texas School Book Depository. Officer Marrion Baker, a motorcycle officer in the motorcade, was sure the shots had come from the Book Depository. He ran into the building. Along with Roy Truly, the building manager, he ran upstairs. As they went up, Oswald made his way down to the second floor.

The three men met for a brief moment in the lunchroom. When Truly identified Oswald as an employee, Officer Baker let him pass. (Baker later noted that Oswald wasn't out of breath and seemed calm.)

Oswald immediately left the building. It was about 12:33 P.M.

Television and radio newscasters were already reporting the shots.

By 12:37 P.M., the police had sealed the Book Depository. Employees gathered on the first floor, but it was too late. Oswald was on a bus headed for Oak Cliff, where he lived during the week. Four blocks after boarding the bus, he got off and took a taxi to his rented room, where everyone knew him as O. H. Lee. Earlene Roberts, the housekeeper, tried to tell "Mr. Lee" what had happened, but he didn't stop to listen. In his room, Oswald changed his jacket and put a .38-caliber pistol in his pocket. Then he left the house on foot.

Back at the Book Depository, the manager took roll and noticed that Oswald was missing. When officers learned that Oswald fit the eyewitness descriptions, he became the first suspect. Police transmitted his description to the street patrols: white male, about five feet six inches, 150 pounds, twenty-four years old, dark hair, wearing a dark jacket.

Agent Clint Hill quickly made his way to the car and climbed onto the trunk.

In shock, Jackie also tried to climb onto the trunk. Later, she claimed to have no memory of doing so. Some suggest she was trying to help Hill into the car.

Meanwhile, at Parkland Hospital, Secret Service agents secured the parking lot and the emergency area. Agents tried to remove the president from the car. At first, Jackie Kennedy refused to let go of her husband. Finally, Agent Hill spoke gently to her, but she refused even him. "You know he's dead. Let me alone," she said.[1]

Agents with submachine guns hustled Vice President Johnson and his wife into a secure room inside the hospital. No one knew who had shot the president and governor, or why. Until they knew otherwise, they had to assume that the attack was part of a larger plot. If that was true, the vice president was still in danger.

Finally, Jackie released her husband, and Secret Service agents moved his body to a stretcher. She ran alongside as the agents wheeled the president down a corridor into a trauma room. Everyone could see the blood that stained her white gloves and pink suit.

Inside the trauma room, Dr. Kemp Clark, a neurosurgeon, asked the First Lady if she would prefer to wait outside. She refused to leave.

Dr. Malcolm Perry enlarged a wound just below the president's Adam's apple and inserted a tube, hoping to get air into the president's lungs. The doctors pumped blood into him and inserted a tube into his chest to keep his lungs from collapsing. A machine that measured heart rate showed a flat, straight line. It was hopeless, but the doctors continued to work.

Doris Nelson, a nurse, gently insisted that the First Lady wait outside. Mrs. Kennedy joined Mrs. Connally in the hall, where they waited together.

In the trauma room, Dr. Perry used his fist to knead the president's chest, but the flat line persisted.

Three minutes passed . . . five minutes . . . seven minutes.

Finally, Dr. Perry stepped away from the body.

Jackie returned to the room and stood next to her husband's body. Someone gently pulled down the president's eyelids and covered his body with a clean white sheet. It was 12:46 P.M.

Father Oscar Huber arrived just a few minutes later and performed the sacrament of the last rites. He was the same priest who had caught a glimpse of the president's head less than a half hour earlier. He had gone to the hospital as soon as he heard the news.

Jackie bent over and kissed her husband's ankle. Then she reached under the sheet and held his hand for a moment. At some point, she removed her wedding ring and placed it on one of her husband's fingers.

Back in the hall, Doris Nelson asked the First Lady if she'd like to wash up. Looking down at her bloodstained hands and skirt, she said, "No, I want them to see what they have done."[2]

Soon, the business of returning the new president, Lyndon B. Johnson, to Washington, D.C., took precedence. Ken O'Donnell, one of President Kennedy's assistants, entered the small room where the vice president and his wife were waiting. "Mr. President . . . ," he said. Johnson jolted. Mrs. Johnson gasped and put a gloved hand to her mouth. They were both shocked. It was the first confirmation they had of President Kennedy's death.[3]

Still wearing her bloodstained suit, she watches the casket of her slain husband placed in an ambulance at Andrews Air Force Base in Maryland.

Jackie Kennedy is comforted by John's brother Attorney Gen. Robert Kennedy.

Upstairs in the lobby, reporters were frantic to learn something—anything. Shortly after 1:00 p.m., Malcolm Kilduff, the White House press secretary, briefed them: "President John F. Kennedy died at approximately 1:00 P.M. Central Standard Time today here in Dallas. He died of a gunshot wound in the brain."[4]

Around that time, witnesses saw Oswald about one mile from his rooming house, walking in the direction of Jack Ruby's apartment. The two men lived just 1.3 miles apart. Although Oswald and Ruby were almost neighbors, there's nothing to suggest that they knew each other. Albert Newman suggests that Oswald was on his way across town to assassinate Army General Edwin Walker.[5] (Oswald's wife, Marina, later testified that Oswald had tried to kill Walker in April of 1963.)

Officer J.D. Tippit stopped Oswald, possibly because he fit the assassin's description. A few seconds later, Officer Tippit lay bleeding in the street. Oswald

dropped the spent shells in the grass, reloaded, and walked on. William Scoggins, a taxi driver, heard the shots. He didn't see Oswald pull the trigger because shrubs blocked his view. He did see Oswald leave the scene. Scoggins used the radio in Tippit's patrol car to call for help, but Tippit was already dead. It was 1:16 P.M.

A few minutes later, Johnny Brewer saw Oswald walk by his shoe store. Just about that time, he heard a news report about the slain officer. The newscaster repeated Oswald's description. Brewer stepped outside and watched Oswald step into the Texas Theatre. Brewer followed and talked to Julia Postal, a cashier, who called the police. Within minutes, police entered the theater.

Oswald punched Officer Nick McDonald between the eyes and quickly drew his gun. He pulled the trigger, but the gun didn't go off. Officer McDonald struck back. Then, several officers wrestled Oswald to the ground and handcuffed him. At some point during the scuffle, Oswald said, "Well, it's all over now."[6]

The police knew they had Tippit's killer. They didn't know he was Lee Harvey Oswald, the president's suspected assassin. According to the clock in the theater lobby, it was 1:50 P.M.

While Dallas police officers were wrestling with Oswald, the new president and his wife headed for the airport in an unmarked car. Safely on board Air Force One, Johnson heard newscaster Walter Cronkite announce President Kennedy's death to the world at about 2:00 P.M. For the next several seconds, Cronkite fell silent.

The entire country fell silent. Then, the country wept, openly and unashamed.

In Irving, Ruth Paine and Marina Oswald heard the news. Marina ran to her room and cried. Later, Ruth mentioned to Marina that reporters claimed the assassin had shot from the Book Depository, where Lee worked. In a panic, Marina ran to the garage, where she found the rolled-up blanket in its usual spot. She was relieved.

At police headquarters, Captain Will Fritz learned that their cop killer and the president's assassin were the same man.

At Parkland Hospital, Dr. George Burkley, the president's private physician, and Agent Kellerman argued with Dallas authorities, who refused to

Vice President Lyndon B. Johnson takes the oath of office aboard Air Force One.

Barely two hours had passed since President Kennedy was shot before Vice President Johnson was sworn in as Kennedy's replacement.

release the president's body. Dr. Earl Rose, the Dallas medical examiner, insisted that the body remain in Dallas for an autopsy. Apparently, the federal government had no jurisdiction over the president's body.

Agents surrounded the casket on a stretcher in the hall while Rose and an armed police officer blocked the agents' exit. There was a momentary standoff until District Attorney Henry Wade waived the local law. It was a few minutes past 2:00 P.M.

Once Mrs. Kennedy and President Kennedy's body were on board Air Force One, Lyndon Baines Johnson took the oath of office. He laid his right hand on a Bible held by U.S. District Judge Sarah T. Hughes. Mrs. Johnson stood to his right. Jackie Kennedy stood on his left, in her blood-soaked suit and stockings. It was 2:38 P.M.

The unbelievable had happened. President John F. Kennedy was dead, shot by an assassin. The ordeal was just beginning.

Lee Harvey Oswald was born in New Orleans, Louisiana, on October 18, 1939, to Marguerite Claverie. His father, Robert Edward Lee Oswald, died two months before Lee was born. His mother had trouble taking care of Lee and his two brothers, and they spent some time in an orphanage.

The family moved to Dallas in 1944. Lee was shy. In high school, he got in trouble for fighting. At age sixteen, he supposedly told a friend he would like to kill President Dwight D. Eisenhower. When he was seventeen, he joined the United States Marine Corps. It was there that he learned how to shoot an M-1 rifle.

In 1958, the Marines court-martialed him for having an unregistered gun in his living quarters. They'd have never known about the gun, except that

Oswald as a U.S. Marine

Oswald accidentally shot himself with it. A year later, he was court-martialed again for disobeying a sergeant.

While in the Marine Corps, Oswald became interested in communism and studied Russian. The Marines honorably discharged Oswald in 1959 after he requested a hardship discharge. His mother needed his help at home, he claimed. However, he spent just three days at home with his mother.

Oswald moved to Russia in October of 1959. In September of 1960, the Marines dishonorably discharged him after he renounced his American citizenship.

Unfortunately for Oswald, the Russians weren't impressed with him and denied his request for citizenship. He found their government corrupt. After a while, he was so disappointed that he even tried to commit suicide.

Lee Harvey and Marina

In 1962, he returned to the United States with his Russian wife, Marina, and their baby daughter, June. Oswald was not a good husband. He couldn't keep a job and he often hit his wife.

It wasn't long before Oswald found another communist country to admire—Cuba. In the summer of 1963, he applied for a Cuban visa. He even offered to join Fidel Castro's military forces. Oswald was disappointed when the Cubans didn't want him.

John F. Kennedy Jr. salutes his father's coffin. He turned three the day of his father's funeral.

His sister, Caroline (holding her mother's hand), would turn six just two days later.

While the World Mourns

Air Force One landed in Washington, D.C., around 6:15 P.M. Robert Kennedy, the president's brother and the attorney general of the United States, boarded the plane as soon as it landed. Eight pallbearers followed, but the Secret Service agents wouldn't let the pallbearers help. Robert Kennedy escorted Mrs. Kennedy from the plane.

The nation watched in horror as the elegant Jackie walked out in her bloodstained suit. Her lost expression told the rest of the story. She rode with the body in the ambulance to Bethesda Naval Hospital, where forensic experts performed an autopsy.

Once the president's body and Mrs. Kennedy had left the airfield, President Johnson emerged from the plane. He looked weary and tired.[1] Johnson made a short statement:

> This is a sad time for all people. We have suffered a loss that cannot be weighed. For me it is a deep personal tragedy. I know the world shares the sorrow that Mrs. Kennedy and her family bear. I will do my best. That is all I can do. I ask your help— and God's.[2]

With his wife, President Johnson boarded a helicopter and headed for the White House, where he met with cabinet members. Late that evening, he returned to his home in Maryland.

An honor guard stood outside the morgue while doctors reviewed the president's wounds. Because the Dallas physicians had used the original throat wound to get air into the president's lungs, the doctors at Bethesda couldn't

determine, with complete certainty, the entry and exit wounds. As a rule, an entry wound is small and well defined. The exit wound is usually larger and jagged because the exiting bullet tears the flesh. The autopsy concluded that both shots came from behind the car: "The deceased died of two perforating gunshot wounds inflicted by high velocity projectiles . . . fired from a point behind and somewhat above the deceased."[3]

Friday evening, the police interrogated Oswald several times, but never for very long. They found a military draft card with the name Alek J. Hidell in Oswald's wallet. The suspect denied knowing anyone by that name, nor would he explain why he had the man's card. Later, the police learned that Hidell was the alias Oswald had used to purchase his rifle. He also used this alias to start a chapter of the Fair Play for Cuba Committee, a pro-Fidel Castro organization, in New Orleans.[4]

Shortly before 1:00 A.M., the Dallas police charged Lee Harvey Oswald with the president's murder. He repeatedly denied shooting anyone. During the follow-up press conference, the police mentioned their plan to move Oswald to the county jail in a few days. No one paid much attention to the stocky man acting as a translator for the Israeli press. That man was Jack Ruby.

An ambulance returned President Kennedy's body to the White House at 4:20 A.M. Sailors, marines, and airmen carried the casket inside to the East Room, where Abraham Lincoln had also lain in state. An honor guard representing all branches of the armed services stood at attention, facing the casket.

The White House was a solemn but busy place Saturday, November 23, 1963. Family members and dignitaries arrived in large numbers to pay their last respects to President Kennedy.

Late Saturday night, the Dallas Federal Bureau of Investigation (FBI) received an anonymous phone call. The caller warned that someone planned to assassinate Oswald when the police moved him the next morning.

Sunday afternoon, at 12:20 P.M., a horse-drawn caisson carried the president's flag-draped coffin down Pennsylvania Avenue to the Senate Rotunda. A drum kept the pace for the slow procession at just 100 steps per minute.[5] During a short service, the president's family and friends spoke lovingly of him. Afterward, mourners stood for hours in the rain to pay their respects.

Back in Dallas, Jack Ruby left his apartment a little after 11:00 A.M. He stopped by a Western Union office and sent a money order. A time stamp on the receipt reads 11:17 A.M.[6] (With the one-hour time difference, this was just about the same time that the caisson began its procession in Washington, D.C.)

The police station was visible from the Western Union office. On his way out, Ruby saw a large crowd, so he walked over. He made his way through the crowd to the basement as detectives escorted Oswald into the parking garage. The area was brightly lit by camera lights because television crews were broadcasting the move live.

Viewers across the nation watched as Jack Ruby walked right up to Oswald and shouted, "You killed my president, you rat!"[7] Then Ruby shoved a pistol into Oswald's stomach and fired at point-blank range.

Police immediately wrestled Ruby to the ground and arrested him.

Security was so lax when they moved Lee Harvey Oswald that Ruby was able to walk right up to Oswald and shoot him dead.

Jack Ruby shot Lee Harvey Oswald in the basement of the Dallas jail.

Doctors at Parkland Hospital pronounced Oswald dead Sunday, November 24, 1963, at 1:07 P.M.

A stunned nation watched the president's funeral the next day, Monday, November 25, 1963. The horse-drawn caisson left the Capitol building at 11:00 A.M. A solemn drumbeat prodded the participants forward, just as the day before. A young soldier led a riderless horse in front of the caisson. A riderless horse is a traditional symbol of a fallen leader. Jackie Kennedy and the president's brothers, Robert and Edward, walked behind the caisson. Representatives from ninety-two countries attended the funeral at St. Matthew's Cathedral.[8]

After the funeral Mass, an honor guard carried the casket down the steps of the cathedral. A band played "Hail to the Chief" one last time for President Kennedy. As the casket passed the family, Jackie leaned forward and spoke to her young son. He stepped forward and saluted his father, in what would become one of the most memorable moments of the entire weekend. It was John Jr.'s third birthday.

At Arlington National Cemetery, the honor guard removed the flag from the president's casket. In a special ceremony, members of the honor guard meticulously folded the flag and presented it to his widow.

An eternal flame marks the president's final resting place as a reminder to the world that John F. Kennedy gave his life for his country. Before leaving the White House, Jackie Kennedy had her husband's name and vital statistics chiseled on the marble mantel of his bedroom.

The funerals for Officer J.D. Tippit and Lee Harvey Oswald were the same day. Over 1,000 mourners attended Tippit's funeral. Three attended Oswald's: his wife, his mother, and his older brother, Robert.

Jack Ruby was tried on February 17, 1964, for the murder of Lee Harvey Oswald. His lawyer claimed that Ruby suffered from psychomotor epilepsy, a neurological disease. He explained to the jury that a serious shock can trigger a violent outburst. The president's assassination was just such a trigger, Ruby's lawyer argued. The jury deliberated for an hour and found him guilty. They recommended the death penalty.

Anyone hoping that the trial would offer some insight into Oswald's motives for killing the president was disappointed. Many thought that Ruby was part of a larger plot to kill the president. When Oswald was arrested, Ruby killed him to keep him from telling what he knew of the conspiracy. Ruby knew he was dying of cancer so had little to lose. In return for killing Oswald, the Mafia agreed to take care of Ruby's elderly mother. However, there's no evidence to prove any of this is true.

Ruby took a lie-detector test for the Warren Commission on July 18, 1964. The commission's report confirmed Ruby's story: He was *not* part of any plot or conspiracy.

In 1966, the Texas Court of Criminal Appeals granted Ruby a new trial. They chose Wichita Falls, Texas, as the new trial site.

In December of 1966, the Wichita Falls sheriff refused to move Ruby because he was sick. Doctors at Parkland Hospital diagnosed Ruby with cancer. Before Ruby could stand trial again, he died on January 3, 1967, when a blood clot in his leg broke free and traveled to his lung. (Many sources claim he died of cancer.)

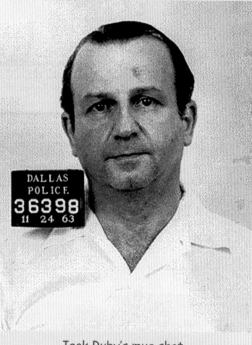

While in prison, Ruby repeatedly asked to go to Washington. Some believe he didn't feel safe telling the truth about the conspiracy in Texas. Ruby's testimony seems to imply the opposite: He wanted to go to Washington to clear himself of a conspiracy. Publicly, Ruby insisted to his dying day that he was not part of a conspiracy to kill the president.

Jack Ruby's mug shot

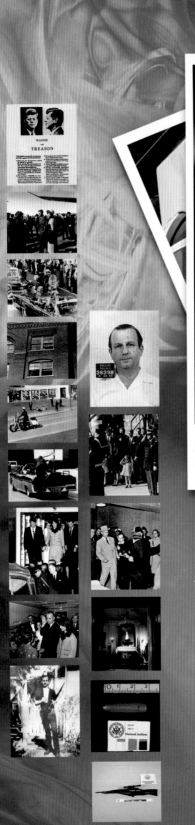

President John F. Kennedy's casket lay in state until his funeral.

An honor guard stood vigil around the clock.

Truth and Speculation

One of President Johnson's first acts as president was to appoint a committee to learn as much as they could about Kennedy's assassination. Chief Justice Earl Warren headed the commission, which became known as the Warren Commission. Other members were senators, congressmen, and lawyers.

The commission worked for ten months. They heard testimony from 552 witnesses. The FBI and Secret Service interviewed 26,550 people.[1] The commission examined the Zapruder film dozens of times; that film was the only known recording of the shooting. The commission re-created the event several times.

The report, released on September 24, 1964, comprised twenty-six volumes and concluded that Lee Harvey Oswald acted alone to kill President John F. Kennedy:

> The Commission has found no evidence that Oswald was involved with any person or group in a conspiracy . . . if there is any such evidence, it has been beyond the reach of all the investigative agencies and resources of the United States and has not come to the attention of the Commission.[2]

Furthermore, the commission concluded that Oswald was motivated by frustration, envy, and a lust for fame and recognition.[3]

While the Warren Commission concluded that Oswald acted alone, it was not able to determine his motive. They did isolate a few factors that might have influenced him:

• He resented authority and was unable to function in society.

- He wasn't able to maintain meaningful relationships with other people.
- He was violent. He had tried to kill General Edwin Walker seven months earlier. Oswald confided to Marina, his wife, that he had taken a sniper shot at the general on April 10, 1963. In addition, he often beat his wife.
- He was a communist, although he seemed just as unsuccessful and unhappy in Russia as he was in the United States.

The report suggests that Oswald wanted to kill someone famous. It doesn't explain why he chose politicians over other public figures.

One of the members of the Warren Commission, Senator Richard B. Russell of Georgia, wasn't satisfied with the report's findings. He objected to the original wording that there had been *no* conspiracy, and refused to sign the report. Earl Warren rewrote the concluding remarks, and then Russell signed.

According to the report, Marina Oswald testified that her husband was devoted to the Cuban cause and that she supported him. As a Russian, she had been taught that Fidel Castro was a benevolent leader who improved living conditions for his people. She didn't understand why Americans didn't like Castro.[4]

In May of 1963, Oswald had applied for admission to the Fair Play for Cuba Committee based in New York City.[5] At the time, he was living in New Orleans and working at a coffee-canning factory. It appears that he worked to open a chapter of the FPCC in New Orleans, although he was unsuccessful. About the same time, Oswald traveled to Mexico with the intentions of traveling on to Cuba. The Cuban consulate in Mexico refused his request.

Marina also testified that Oswald threatened to kill former Vice President Richard Nixon in April of 1963 after Nixon publicly condemned the Cuban regime. According to Marina, Oswald told her that Nixon was in town and he was going to see him. When he picked up his pistol, she confronted him. They fought, and Marina locked him in the bathroom, where he spent most of the day. She believed that the whole event was an act to scare her so that she would return to Russia.

General Walker, Vice President Nixon, and President Kennedy had little in common politically. However, all three were outspoken opponents of

the Cuban government under Fidel Castro. Some have used this information to suggest the Cubans assassinated President Kennedy, but there is no evidence to substantiate that. What these three events do present is a possible motive for Oswald.

On November 18, 1963, just days before his visit to Dallas, President Kennedy publicly criticized Castro for betraying the ideals of the Cuban Revolution.[6]

The Warren Commission's statements on the evidence were also somewhat controversial. According to the Warren Report, Oswald shot three bullets. The first bullet missed its target and struck the curb. The second bullet struck both Kennedy and Connally. The third bullet struck Kennedy's head. Several witnesses claimed to have heard four shots, not three. They also claimed that the shots varied in loudness. Some used these claims to suggest there was more than one shooter.

The commission's single-bullet theory produced the largest outcry of doubt. The commission said that the second bullet inflicted wounds to both Kennedy and Connally. The Zapruder film shows that the men were wounded within 1.6 seconds of each other. Oswald needed 2.3 seconds between each shot.[7] Either one bullet struck both men, or there were two shooters. Since people found the one-bullet theory difficult to believe, they insisted there must have been more than one shooter, and that meant there was a conspiracy.

Governor Connally's physical reaction to the shot that hit him supports the commission's theory. He heard the first shot and instinctively turned in the direction of the sound—to the right. Almost immediately, he turned to his left to check on the president. The second shot was fired and Kennedy grasped his throat. At the same time, the governor jerked as though something slammed into his back.[8] There was no discernible time between both impacts—only the second necessary for the bullet to travel the few feet from the president's chest to the governor's back. Despite the commission's explanation, many people doubt the single-bullet theory.

In addition, the autopsy report couldn't distinguish, with 100 percent certainty, between the entry and exit wounds. The doctors at Parkland Hospital had enlarged the wound just below the president's Adam's apple. In doing so, they damaged forensic evidence.

CE 399
FBI C1

National Archives

One bullet was found on a stretcher at Parkland Memorial Hospital.

The Warren Commission claimed that this lead-core 6.5-mm rifle bullet was the "single bullet" that passed through Kennedy's neck and caused all of Connally's wounds (chest, wrist, and thigh).

Close examination of the president's clothing was supposed to put most of this controversy to rest. The FBI found a small hole in the back of his suit coat and shirt, characteristic of an entry hole. In addition, the fibers around the hole were bent inward. The presumed exit hole produced a slit, which is characteristic of an exit hole, as noted by J. Edgar Hoover, the director of the FBI: "[Examination] revealed a small hole in the back of his coat and shirt and a slit characteristic of the exit hole below the collar button. A bullet hole in the left side of the tie knot, possibly caused by the same projectile which passed through the shirt, also was noted."[9] The president's clothes are now in the National Archives.

Many mistakes were made early in the discovery process. For instance, during a press conference shortly after the president died, Dr. Malcolm Perry was reported to have said that the head wound's entry point was in the front of

the head. Later, Perry testified that he did *not* say that. Perry further testified that he found several mistakes and misstatements in the published reports.[10]

Another oversight was the commission's inability to explain witness accounts of hearing gunfire from the grassy knoll to the right of the president's car. Most eyewitnesses said the shots came from the Book Depository because of what they heard, not what they saw. A few, however, thought the sounds came from the grassy knoll. One of those few was Agent Sorrels, who was riding in the lead car directly in front of the presidential limousine. He later told a friend that the shots came from the grassy knoll.[11]

Immediately following the shots, police climbed a fence at the top of the knoll and searched the area. They found no bullet casings or footprints.

One explanation for the discrepancy in what the witnesses heard is the physics of the sound produced by the rifle. That sound bounced off the three walls surrounding Dealey Plaza, distorting it. At best, earshot testimony was unreliable.

One of the most bizarre statements came from Oswald's mother, Marguerite Oswald, who claimed that the president was already dying and if Oswald indeed shot him, he did so as an act of kindness.

Another interesting oversight is that no one on the commission actually saw or studied the autopsy X-rays and photographs: The Kennedy family wouldn't turn them over. Eventually, the family finally placed them in the National Archives on November 1, 1966. However, no one was allowed to view or study them for at least five years—that was the family's condition for contributing the evidence to the archives.

It's unusual that the government allowed the family to keep such important evidence. Equally disturbing is the commission's failure to insist on seeing the X-rays and photographs. John J. McCloy, a member of the commission, explained, "We were perhaps a little oversensitive to what we understood were the sensitivities of the Kennedy family."[12] In other words, the Kennedys didn't want strangers viewing the horrific images, and the commission went along with their wishes.

In 1979, a second commission appointed by Congress reached a different conclusion from the Warren Commission. The second commission concluded that Oswald was one of the gunmen, but that others—specifically, the

Mafia—might have been involved. Robert Kennedy, as attorney general of the United States, had announced his intentions to get tough on organized crime (the Mafia). Still, the commission had no evidence to support such a conspiracy.

Many still believe that Oswald didn't act alone. It is difficult for people to accept that just one man could have such a huge impact on the world. Despite the lack of evidence to support a conspiracy, people still choose to believe in one.

Nonetheless, it has been hard for many Americans to accept that Oswald acted alone. The Warren Report came under attack immediately. Critics accused the commission of a cover-up because they believed Americans couldn't handle the truth of a larger conspiracy.

Whether the commission did a good job is subjective. They couldn't ask Oswald for the truth, and there was no forensic evidence to point to a conspiracy. That doesn't stop people from speculating. Some even accuse the commission of burying evidence of a conspiracy.

If Oswald didn't act alone, who helped him? Some suggest that the Cuban government assassinated President Kennedy. A rumor exists that the Central Intelligence Agency (CIA) tried to assassinate Fidel Castro and failed. The Cubans retaliated and succeeded with Oswald's help.

Another theory involves the Vietnam War. Kennedy had advisers and troops in Vietnam. Although his plan was never made public, he planned to withdraw American troops and support from the conflict. There were those who opposed that move—most of them were making a lot of money off the war by selling weapons and other goods to the military. Money can be a strong motivator.

There's no evidence, at least not in either report, that proves that anyone other than Oswald was a party to the president's death.

President John F. Kennedy was loved by many Americans. Many believed his goals were ambitious and noble, but he also had a lot of enemies. Neither commission really answered the question of why President Kennedy was assassinated. The one thing we can all be certain of is this: His assassination was a tragic event that shocked the entire world. The mystery surrounding John F. Kennedy's death is just as compelling now as it was when it happened more than forty years ago.

According to the Warren Report, Lee Harvey Oswald was guilty, even though there was no trial, for the following reasons:

- He purchased the rifle used to kill President Kennedy and wound Governor Connally.
- He carried the rifle to the Book Depository on the morning of the assassination.
- He was present at the Book Depository window at the time of the assassination.
- He killed Dallas police officer J.D. Tippit in an attempt to escape.
- He resisted arrest by drawing a loaded pistol and trying to shoot another Dallas police officer.
- He lied to police after his arrest.
- He attempted to kill General Edwin Walker in April of 1963.
- He possessed the shooting skill to commit the assassination.

Based on these findings, the commission concluded that Oswald was the president's assassin.

Police found Oswald's Mannlicher-Carcano rifle on the sixth floor of the Book Depository. One live shell was in the chamber. Three empty cartridge cases lay on a southeast windowsill—the one from which Oswald fired.

Investigators traced Oswald's rifle and revolver (the one he used to kill Officer Tippit) to a post office box rented by Alek Hidell, Oswald's alias. Fibers found on the rifle matched the

Mannlicher-Carcano rifle owned by Lee Harvey Oswald and allegedly used to assassinate President John F. Kennedy

blanket in Ruth Paine's garage. Marina testified that her husband kept his rifle in that blanket. They found Oswald's partial palm print on the rifle. Bullet fragments removed from the limousine and the two victims matched the spent shells.

Police found gunpowder residue on Oswald's hands, which proves that he fired a revolver. They did not find residue on his cheeks, which would have indicated he had shot a rifle. However, in 1963, tests for gunpowder residue were unreliable. At that time, the absence of residue on his cheeks wasn't proof that Oswald had *not* fired the rifle.

Chronology

1917	John F. Kennedy is born in Brookline, Massachusetts, on May 29.
1939	Lee Harvey Oswald is born on October 18 in New Orleans, Louisiana.
1940	Kennedy graduates from Harvard University and joins the United States Navy.
1943	Kennedy's PT (Patrol Torpedo) boat is cut in two by a Japanese ship. Kennedy is injured but leads the crew to safety. He receives a Purple Heart and the Navy and Marine Corps Medal for heroism.
1944	The Oswald family moves to Dallas, Texas.
1946	Kennedy runs for U.S. Congress and wins.
1952	He runs for U.S. Senate and wins.
1953	Kennedy marries Jacqueline Bouvier on September 12.
1955	Kennedy writes the book *Profiles in Courage*.
1956	Oswald joins the United States Marine Corps at the age of seventeen.
1957	The Pulitzer Prize is awarded to Kennedy for *Profiles in Courage*.
1958	Kennedy is reelected to the Senate. Oswald is court-martialed.
1959	Oswald is honorably discharged from the United States Marine Corps, citing hardship.
1960	Democratic Party nominates Kennedy for president. Kennedy is elected the thirty-fifth president of the United States. Oswald moves to Russia.
1961	Kennedy is inaugurated on January 20. The Bay of Pigs invasion fails on April 17.
1962	The United States and the Soviet Union face off over Cuban missiles. Oswald returns to the United States with his wife, Marina, and their daughter, June.
1963	United States signs Limited Nuclear Test Ban Treaty with the Soviet Union and Great Britain in August. Oswald takes a shot at General Edwin Walker, but misses, on April 10. About the same time, Oswald threatens to kill former Vice President Richard Nixon. Kennedy introduces the Civil Rights Bill to Congress. Oswald applies for a visa to Cuba but is denied. Kennedy criticizes Castro publicly on November 18. Kennedy is assassinated by Lee Harvey Oswald on November 22. Lee Harvey Oswald is arrested that day for the murder. Jack Ruby shoots and kills Oswald on November 24. Kennedy is buried at Arlington National Cemetery on November 25.
1964	The Warren Commission reports on the assassination on September 24. Jack Ruby's trial begins on February 17.
1966	Texas Court of Criminal Appeals grants Ruby a new trial. Kennedy family turns the president's autopsy X-rays and photographs over to the National Archives on November 1.
1967	Jack Ruby dies in Parkland Hospital.
1979	Select Committee on Assassinations reports that Kennedy's assassination probably involved at least two gunmen.
1998	The National Archives releases the autopsy reports and trial records regarding the Kennedy assassination.

Chronology of
November 22 through
November 25, 1963

All times are central standard time (CST) unless noted as eastern standard time (EST).

November 22

Early A.M.   President Kennedy makes two morning speeches in Fort Worth, Texas. In Dallas, Texas, Lee Harvey Oswald carries a rifle wrapped in paper to work at the Texas School Book Depository.

11:39 A.M.   President Kennedy's party arrives at Love Field in Dallas, Texas.

11:55 A.M.   Kennedy's motorcade leaves Love Field and begins its journey through the streets of Dallas.

12:30 P.M.   Kennedy's presidential limousine turns left onto Elm Street in front of the Texas School Book Depository building. Abraham Zapruder starts filming the motorcade.

12:30 P.M.   Kennedy is shot.

12:32 P.M.   Officer Marrion Baker, Roy Truly, and Oswald meet on the second floor of the Book Depository building.

12:33 P.M.   Oswald leaves the Book Depository building.

12:34 P.M.   Dallas police enter the Book Depository building.

12:37 P.M.   Dallas police seal the Book Depository building.

12:45 P.M.   Police release a description of the suspected shooter.

12:46 P.M.   A doctor covers President Kennedy's body with a white sheet, indicating he is dead.

1:00 P.M.   Kennedy is officially pronounced dead. Malcolm Kilduff, the White House press secretary, makes the announcement to the press a little after 1:30 p.m.

1:16 P.M.   William Scoggins radios for help after Oswald shoots and kills Officer J.D. Tippit.

1:50 P.M.   Police arrest Lee Harvey Oswald at the Texas Theatre.

2:00 P.M.   Walter Cronkite announces the death of the president to the world.

2:38 P.M.   Vice President Lyndon B. Johnson is sworn in as president aboard Air Force One.

6:15 P.M. EST   Air Force One lands in Washington, D.C.

November 23

1:00 A.M.   Dallas police charge Oswald with the president's murder.

4:20 A.M. EST   An honor guard carries the president's body into the East Room of the White House. Throughout the day, friends and family pay their last respects to the president.

November 24

11:00 A.M.   Jack Ruby leaves his apartment.

11:17 A.M.   Ruby purchases a money order.

12:20 P.M. EST	Procession to move the president's body to the Senate Rotunda begins. About the same time in Dallas, Texas, Ruby shoots Oswald.
1:07 P.M.	Doctors pronounce Lee Harvey Oswald dead.

November 25

11:00 A.M. EST	Procession to move the president's body to St. Matthew's Cathedral begins.

Timeline in History

1941	Japanese forces attack Pearl Harbor in Hawaii on December 7. The United States declares war on Japan on December 8 and enters World War II.
1945	The United States drops nuclear bomb on Hiroshima, Japan, on August 6. Japan surrenders, ending World War II, on August 14.
1961	Freedom Riders go to Montgomery, Alabama, in May. East Germany builds the Berlin Wall in August.
1962	John Glenn is the first American to orbit Earth. The first Telstar satellite relays television programs between Europe and the United States. Edward Kennedy is elected to the U.S. Senate.
1963	More than 200,000 people participate in the Freedom March on Washington, D.C., for civil rights, on August 28.
1964	The Civil Rights Act is passed.
1965	President Lyndon Johnson escalates United States involvement in Vietnam by sending more troops.
1968	Martin Luther King Jr. is assassinated in Memphis, Tennessee, on April 4. Robert Kennedy is assassinated in Los Angeles, California, on June 5.
1969	Neil Armstrong is first American to walk on the moon on July 20.
1973	The last American troops leave Vietnam.
1989	Caroline Kennedy founds the Profile in Courage Awards to honor public officials, in honor of her father.
1994	Jacqueline Kennedy Onassis dies of cancer on May 19. She is buried at Arlington National Cemetery, next to John F. Kennedy.
1999	John F. Kennedy Jr., his wife Carolyn Bessette Kennedy, and his sister-in-law Lauren G. Bessette are killed in a plane crash on July 16.
2000	Caroline Kennedy addresses the 2000 Democratic Convention.
2007	Edward Kennedy continues to head several committees as a U.S. Senator.

Chapter Notes

Chapter 1   A Minute in Dallas

1. Jim Bishop, *The Day Kennedy Was Shot* (New York: Funk & Wagnalls, 1968), p. 173.

2. Ibid.

3. Ibid., p. 174.

4. Ibid., p. 175.

5. Ibid., p. 178.

6. Ibid., p. 179.

7. U.S. Department of Labor, *History of Federal Minimum Wage Rates Under the Fair Labor Standards Act, 1938–2007* http://www.dol.gov/esa/minwage/chart.htm

Chapter 2   Friday Morning

1. Jim Bishop, *The Day Kennedy Was Shot* (New York: Funk & Wagnalls, 1968), p. 12.

2. Albert H. Newman, *The Assassination of John F. Kennedy: The Reasons Why* (New York: Clarkson Potter, 1970), p. 527.

3. Bishop, p. 154.

4. Ibid., p. 171.

5. Art Simon, *Dangerous Knowledge: The JFK Assassination in Art and Film* (Philadelphia, Pennsylvania: Temple University Press, 1996), p. 36.

6. Ibid., p. 39.

7. Ibid., p. 40.

8. Ibid., p. 49.

Chapter 3   The Aftermath

1. Jim Bishop, *The Day Kennedy Was Shot* (New York: Funk & Wagnalls, 1968), p. 200.

2. Ibid., p. 226.

3. Ibid., p. 246.

4. Relman Morin, *Assassination: The Death of President John F. Kennedy* (New York: New American Library, 1968), p. 75.

5. Albert H. Newman, *The Assassination of John F. Kennedy: The Reasons Why* (New York: Clarkson Potter, 1970), p. 545.

6. Morin, p. 102.

Chapter 4   While the World Mourns

1. Relman Morin, *Assassination: The Death of President John F. Kennedy* (New York: New American Library, 1968), p. 137.

2. Ibid.

3. Ibid., p. 142.

4. Albert H. Newman, *The Assassination of John F. Kennedy: The Reasons Why* (New York: Clarkson Potter, 1970), p. 383.

5. Ibid., p. 146.

6. Ibid., p. 160.

7. Gerald Posner, *Case Closed: Lee Harvey Oswald and the Assassination of JFK* (New York: Random House, 1993), p. 397.

8. Morin, p. 149.

Chapter 5   Truth and Speculation

1. Relman Morin, *Assassination: The Death of President John F. Kennedy* (New York: New American Library, 1968), p. 177.

2. Ibid.

3. Robert B. Semple Jr., editor, *Four Days in November: The Original Coverage of the John F. Kennedy Assassination by the Staff of* The New York Times, introduction by Tom Wicker (New York: St. Martin's Press, 2003), p. 9.

4. Albert H. Newman, *The Assassination of John F. Kennedy: The Reasons Why* (New York: Clarkson Potter, 1970), p. 27.

5. Ibid., p. 23.

6. Ibid., p. 357.

7. Morin, p. 187.

8. Semple, p. 681.

9. Morin, p. 188.

10. Ibid., p. 187.

11. William E. Scott, *November 22, 1963: A Reference Guide to the JFK Assassination* (Lanham, Maryland: University Press of America, 1999), p. 61.

12. Morin, p. 189.

Glossary

assassinate (uh-SAA-sih-nayt)
To murder a prominent person, usually for political or religious purposes.

attorney general (uh-TUR-nee JEN-ur-uhl)
The chief law officer of the United States government.

autopsy (AW-top-zee)
An examination of a corpse to discover the cause of death.

caisson (KAY-son)
A two-wheeled wagon drawn by horses, usually used to move ammunition.

campaign (kam-PAYN)
A series of public meetings, speeches, and debates where a candidate for public office makes his or her goals known.

civil rights (SIH-vul RYTS)
Rights belonging to individuals by virtue of their citizenship.

cold war
A dispute between Eastern and Western countries during the last half of the twentieth century.

communism (KAH-myoo-nih-zum)
A social and economic system in which the government owns everything and distributes goods and necessities to the people.

conspiracy (kun-SPEER-uh-see)
A secret agreement between two or more people to commit an act, usually an illegal one.

court-martial (KORT MAR-shul)
Disciplinary action taken by a military court against a member of the military.

electoral (ee-LEK-tor-ul)
The votes cast by each state in a presidential election, based on its population.

FBI
The Federal Bureau of Investigation; the U.S. government agency that investigates federal crimes.

forensic (fuh-REN-zik)
Relating to the use of scientific knowledge to solve legal problems.

involuntary (in-VAH-lun-tay-ree)
Not voluntary; not under thoughtful control.

last rites
Sacred ceremony performed just before a person dies or at the time of death; part of the Roman Catholic faith.

lying in state
Ceremony where a person's body is available for public viewing or paying of last respects, usually of an important public figure.

Mafia (MAH-fee-uh)
Secret society that engages in illegal activities.

meticulous (muh-TIK-yoo-lus)
Careful and precise.

morgue (MORG)
Where dead bodies are kept temporarily, usually in a hospital.

motorcade (MOH-tur-kayd)
A parade of vehicles.

pallbearer (PAHL-bayr-er)
Someone who helps carry a casket.

platform
A plan of action to achieve a specific goal or set of goals.

psychomotor epilepsy (SY-koh-moh-ter EP-ih-lep-see)
A neurological disorder where the patient loses control of his or her body; accompanied by phantom sensory sensations, amnesia, and emotional outbursts.

renounce (ree-NOWNS)
To disown.

rotunda (roh-TUN-duh)
A round building or hall, usually with a domed roof.

running board
A narrow footboard under and beside the door of a vehicle.

Secret Service
The government agency in charge of protecting the president, his family, and aides.

segregation (seg-rih-GAY-shun)
To separate by some category such as race or gender.

trachea (TRAY-kee-ah)
The passageway that allows air to flow into the lungs.

Further Reading

For Young Adults
Donnelly, Judy. *Who Shot the President? The Death of John F. Kennedy*. New York: Random House, 1988.
Hampton, Wilborn. *Kennedy Assassinated! The World Mourns: A Reporter's Story*. Cambridge, Massachusetts: Candlewick Press, 1997.
Hossell, Karen Price. *The Assassination of John F. Kennedy: Death of the New Frontier*. Chicago: Heinemann Library, 2002.
Spencer, Lauren. *The Assassination of John F. Kennedy*. New York: Rosen Publishing, 2002.
Swisher, Clarice, editor. *John F. Kennedy*. San Diego, California: Greenhaven Press, 2000.

Works Consulted
Bishop, Jim. *The Day Kennedy Was Shot*. New York: Funk & Wagnalls, 1968.
Mailer, Norman. *Oswald's Tale: An American Mystery*. New York: Random House, 1995.
Morin, Relman. *Assassination: The Death of President John F. Kennedy*. New York: New American Library, 1968.
Newman, Albert H. *The Assassination of John F. Kennedy: The Reasons Why*. New York: Clarkson Potter, 1970.

Posner, Gerald. *Case Closed: Lee Harvey Oswald and the Assassination of JFK*. New York: Random House, 1993.
Scott, William E. *November 22, 1963: A Reference Guide to the JFK Assassination*. Lanham, Maryland: University Press of America, 1999.
Semple, Robert B., Jr., editor. *Four Days in November: The Original Coverage of the John F. Kennedy Assassination by the Staff of* The New York Times. Introduction by Tom Wicker. New York: St. Martin's Press, 2003.
Simon, Art. *Dangerous Knowledge: The JFK Assassination in Art and Film*. Philadelphia: Temple University Press, 1996.

On the Internet
John F. Kennedy Presidential Library & Museum
http://www.jfklibrary.org

National Park Service: *John Fitzgerald Kennedy National Historic Site*
http://www.nps.gov/jofi

The Sixth Floor Museum at Dealey Plaza
http://www.jfk.org

Index